Time Management for Teachers

IAN NELSON

**KOGAN
PAGE**

London • Philadelphia

First published in 1995

Kogan Page Limited
120 Pentonville Road
London N1 9JN

British Library Cataloguing in Publication Data

A CIP record for this book is available from the British Library.

ISBN 0 7494 1730 7

Typeset by Saxon Graphics Ltd, Derby
Printed and bound in Great Britain by Biddles Ltd, Guildford and King's Lynn

Contents

1. **Why Time Management for Teachers?**   1
   How effectively do you manage your time?   3

2. **Where Does your Time Go?**   8
   Analysis of time usage over a full week   8
   Analysis of time usage in the working week   10
   Time-logs   11
   Time-log for a full day   12
   Time-log for a lesson   14

3. **Identifying Timewasters**   16

4. **Planning**   19
   Long-term planning   19
   Medium-term planning   22
   Short-term planning   23
   Prioritizing tasks   26
   Prime time   27
   Urgent or important   28

5. **Organization**   30
   Classroom organization   30
   Getting started   30
   Teaching   31
   Giving out books and collecting them back   34
   Giving instructions   36
   Keeping order   38
   Marking work and assessing pupil performance   39
   Assessing the effectiveness of classroom organization   40
   Organizing non-teaching tasks   41

Contents

6. **Paperwork**   **43**
   Handling incoming paperwork   44
   Act on it   45
   Passing it on   46
   Filing it   46
   Binning it   48

7. **Meetings**   **49**
   Reasons for meetings   51
   Organizing effective meetings   53
   Why meetings fail   54
   Planning a meeting   55
   Assessing the need for a meeting   57
   Who should attend your meeting?   59
   The agenda   60
   Meeting action notes   63
   Leading meetings effectively   66
   Rules for effective chairing of meetings   67
   Being an effective participant in meetings   70
   Rules for being an effective meetings participant   71

8. **Summary and Review**   **73**

CHAPTER I

Why Time Management for Teachers?

Teachers have never been under so much pressure to manage their time efficiently as they are today. The pace and extent of recent changes have brought so much extra work that most teachers complain bitterly that there are no longer enough hours in the day to do their job properly.

They have to be familiar with National Curriculum requirements and all the revisions and statutory requirements for assessment, recording and reporting. This is on top of:

- teaching five hours or so each day
- preparing the work
- marking
- mounting and displaying work
- keeping accurate records of both subject coverage and pupil achievement
- attending staff meetings, parents' meetings, cluster meetings
- attending courses and workshops
- administering a department or curriculum area, etc.

Added to that, the new inspection system includes judgements about the efficiency of the school. Part 4 of the OFSTED handbook for inspection of schools requires inspectors to 'judge how well teachers use their time and expertise' (page 13, section 4). Inspectors have to reach judgements on the value for money provided by the school, taking into account a range of factors including the catchment area, the school's budget, and the standards achieved.

Local management of schools has also increased the burden on teachers, as they have to take far more responsibility for both day-to-day and longer-term budgeting, making decisions on how much to allocate to which headings to ensure the greatest benefits for their pupils. The more effectively teachers use their time the better value for money the school provides. The chart below enables you to work out the cost of your time. From it you can see the real cost of, say, a meeting lasting an hour, a half-hour looking for some papers that you desperately need, or a full-day course. The table is based on a working day of seven hours over 238 days a year. Poor time management actually costs money and you can work out the cost of time wasted by reference to the table.

Salary	5 mins	15 mins	1 hour	1 day
£35,000	£1.75	£5.25	£21.00	£147
£30,000	£1.50	£4.50	£18.00	£126
£25,000	£1.25	£3.75	£15.00	£105
£20,000	£1.00	£3.00	£12.00	£84
£15,000	£0.75	£2.25	£9.00	£63
£10,000	£0.50	£1.50	£6.00	£42

All teachers want to provide the best possible education for their pupils and it stands to reason that tired and overworked teachers are less effective than those with stronger time-management skills who are not as tired and overworked. Time management does pay dividends in terms of improving standards of achievement in the classroom. The more organized and effective you are, the more your pupils learn and the better the results the school achieves.

Increasingly teachers are expected to take on extra responsibility. This is sometimes rewarded with a salary increase (though not always these days) but is rarely rewarded with non-contact time, particularly in the primary school where you will still have a full class teaching timetable alongside your extra responsibilities. Most deputy heads in primary schools still have a full-time class teaching responsibility, and in the smaller schools the head too will have a substantial teaching commitment.

Most books on time management to date have been aimed at people who work in the business world; none has addressed the issue of how to manage your time when around five hours a day is spent in front of a class of pupils. This book does address that issue and, alongside the practical suggestions for time management for those periods of the day when you are free from pupils, it will also offer ideas for greater classroom time management.

The first stage in becoming more effective at managing time is to find out where it is going at present, which is the subject of the next chapter. Before we go on to an analysis of how you use your time at present though, try working through the following questionnaire to see how serious your time management problems are. The questionnaire is arranged in four sections.

How effectively do you manage your time?

I do this   always   often   rarely   never

Planning

1. Plan my lessons
2. Plan my whole day
3. Plan a week at a time
4. Arrange tasks in priority order
5. Have a 'to do' list
Set time in my diary for
6. marking
7. planning
8. preparing work
9. mounting work
10. reading
11. writing reports
12. telephone calls

always   often   rarely   never

Organization

1. Arrive late for lessons
2. Arrive late for meetings
3. Work late at school
4. Take work home
5. Have an untidy desk
6. Have an untidy room
7. Lose important papers
8. Miss my favourite TV show
9. Work at weekends
10. Take daily strenuous exercise
11. Take a lunch break
12. Know exactly where everything is

Paperwork

1. Am overwhelmed with papers
2. Deal with correspondence as it arrives
3. Spend time searching for papers
4. Have a clear desk
5. Handle papers several times over
6. Have an effective filing system
7. Let paperwork mount up
8. Pass papers on quickly
9. Generate lots of paperwork
10. Send frequent memos to colleagues
11. Read everything that arrives
12. Prioritise paperwork

Meetings

1. Arrive on time for meetings
2. Have the papers I need
3. Arrive at the wrong meeting
4. Start meetings on time
5. Know what the meeting is about
6. Fall asleep in meetings
7. Finish meetings on time
8. Attend all the meetings I can

always   often   rarely   never

9. Have clear objectives for meetings
10. Have an agenda
11. Allow meetings to over run
12. Know why I am at the meeting.

Results

So how did you do? To find out, total your score in each section, add up your scores as follows:

Planning

In the planning section, score:
3 for each always
2 for each often
1 for each rarely
0 for each never
Total score for planning:

Organization

For questions 1–9 in this section, score:
0 for each always
1 for each often
2 for each rarely
3 for each never
For questions 10–12, score:
3 for each always
2 for each often
1 for each rarely
0 for each never
Total score for organization:

Paperwork

For questions 2, 4, 6, 8 and 12 in this section, score:
3 for each always
2 for often
1 for rarely
0 for never

For questions 1, 3, 5, 7, 9, 10 and 11, score:
0 for always
1 for often
2 for rarely
3 for never
Total score for paperwork:

Meetings
For questions 1, 2, 4, 5, 7, 9, 10 and 12, score:
3 for always
2 for often
1 for rarely
0 for never.
For questions 3, 6, 8 and 11, score:
0 for always
1 for rarely
2 for often
3 for never
Total score for meetings:

Total score for all sections:

Interpreting your score

Add up your score for each section and find your total for the whole questionnaire. If you scored between 120 and 144 you probably do not need this book, always assuming that you have been totally honest of course!

A score between 100 and 120 indicates that you have developed some good time-management techniques but there is still plenty of room for improvement.

A score between 80 and 100 means that you are certainly in need of help and should read the rest of this book in order to use your time more effectively.

A score between 60 and 80 indicates poor time-management skills that prevent you from working as effectively as you might, and the real possibility that you cause your colleagues some problems too!

If you scored below 60 I am surprised that you have managed to read as far as you have done! However, there is always hope, so read on and see how much time you can save by implementing some of the practical ideas that follow.

You will also see from the results in each section whether your problems with time-management are confined to one area or are of a more general nature.

CHAPTER 2
Where Does your Time Go?

Most of us have a pretty good idea of the state of our finances. We know how much we earn and where it goes. If we want to make our money go further so that we can do more with it, like buying a new car, we work out if we can save a bit here or economize there or take out a loan. On occasions, if we desperately need more money (for a special holiday or whatever), we can earn it by working in a bar in the evenings or at weekends, marking exam papers, private tuition or a range of other means.

However, few of us are as aware of where our time goes, even though there is no way of earning extra time should we be nearing an important deadline. We cannot borrow time as easily as we can money. We can only divert time from some other activity to the urgent one. Once a minute has gone we cannot retrieve it. So the first stage in managing your time more effectively is to understand more clearly how you use it at present. Most people assume that they know where their time goes and that their problems arise from overwork. Try this simple exercise to see how clearly you know how you use your time.

Analysis of time usage over a full week

Make a list of the range of activities that you do in a typical week and then allocate the number of hours you think you spend on each in a typical seven-day week. Start with the list given and add activities that are missing.

Activity	Hours spent per week
sleep	
work	
travelling to/from work	
eating	
watching TV	
exercise	
household chores	
recreation	
hygiene	

Total:

To gain a different perspective, and perhaps more accuracy, you could always ask someone close to you, like your partner or spouse, to complete the same activity for you and see whether their perception matches yours! Having added up the hours spent on each activity you should have a total of 168 hours accounted for. If you have more than this you have clearly overestimated how long you spend on some activities, or you have double-counted because you read in the bath and have counted those hours as both hygiene and recreation. If you have less than the 168 hours accounted for, you have underestimated the amount of time spent on some activities, or you have no need of this book, or you have some explaining to do to your partner!

From the results of a simple exercise like this you can get some insight into where you think your time is going and, even at this stage, you can start considering ways of managing it better. However, before we look at ways of managing time better we need to focus more closely on how we use those tracts of time allocated to work.

Just as we have split the week up into separate activities to try to work out where time goes, so we can do the same for the working week. Do the following exercise allocating the number of hours you think you spend on each activity in a normal working week; add any you think are missing.

Analysis of time usage in the working week

Activity	Hours spent per week
teaching	
marking	
preparation	
mounting work	
meetings (scheduled)	
meetings (unscheduled)	
telephone calls in	
telephone calls out	
writing (letters, reports, etc.)	
reading (letters, reports, etc.)	
looking for papers	
filing	
	Total:

You worked out in the first exercise how long you thought you spent working in a typical week, so the total time you get in this exercise should amount to the same. If it does not then you have clearly over- or underestimated the time spent on some activities.

There is one final exercise to complete in this analysis of where you think your time goes. Within a single lesson, you are involved in a number of activities. Estimate how much of the time you spend in lessons is spent on each activity in a normal week. Add any activities that are missing from the following list.

Activity	Hours spent per week
getting started	
teaching	
giving out books, materials, etc.	
giving instructions	
keeping order	
marking	
collecting books in	
checking understanding of instructions	

checking understanding of learning
assessing pupils
clearing up at the end
dismissing classes

Total:

The total time here should be the same as the time you estimated that you spent in teaching in a normal week, unless
you have over- or underestimated how long you spend on
each activity.

Having done these simple self-perception exercises, you
should have some idea of how you think you spend your
time. Even at this stage you can begin to see how you might
alter the balance between activities to help you to be more
effective. If you are serious about improving your time management, however, you will want to check your perception of
where time goes with the reality, through keeping a simple
time-log.

Time-logs

This is the stage when most people say they haven't got time
to keep a log, although they will happily work out where
their money goes when they want to know if they can afford
a new car or whatever. In order to have your new car you
look at your present use of money to see where savings can
be made so that you can afford it. Looking closely at how you
currently spend your time is essential to enable you to start
planning how to save it. The first stage is to devise a simple
time-log to check fairly accurately how your time is being
used now so that you can see where savings might be made.
To keep a time-log involves noting at specified intervals what
you have actually done during that time. The intervals might
be as short as 5 minutes in a lesson or 15 minutes in a full
day time-log. Having totalled the time spent on each activity
you then have a much clearer picture of how much time you
actually spend on each activity compared with your earlier
estimate. The first log is for a full day, although you could

use it for parts of a day. Devising a simple code for each of the activities identified earlier will make it easier to keep.

Time-log for a full day

Time	Activity	Time	Activity
7.00		7.15	
7.30		7.45	
8.00		8.15	
8.30		8.45	
9.00		9.15	
9.30		9.45	
10.00		10.15	
10.30		10.45	
11.00		11.15	
11.30		11.45	
12.00		12.15	
12.30		12.45	
1.00		1.15	
1.30		1.45	
2.00		2.15	
2.30		2.45	
3.00		3.15	
3.30		3.45	
4.00		4.15	
4.30		4.45	
5.00		5.15	
5.30		5.45	
6.00		6.15	
6.30		6.45	
7.00		7.15	
7.30		7.45	
8.00		8.15	
8.30		8.45	
9.00		9.15	
9.30		9.45	
10.00			

Activities	Time spent on each
teaching	
marking	
preparation	
mounting work	
meetings (scheduled)	
meetings (unscheduled)	
telephone calls in	
telephone calls out	
writing (letters, reports etc.)	
reading (letters, reports etc.)	
looking for papers	
playground duty	
filing	
travel	
eating	
coffee breaks	
relaxing	
household chores	

This time-log spans a whole day in quarter-hour intervals. You could adapt it to use it for only parts of the day but the more fully and accurately you keep it the easier it will be to identify your own timewasters and begin to explore ways of combating them.

Some organizations require their workers to keep timesheets of this nature on a regular weekly basis so that they can allocate types of work to particular headings where these are funded by different bodies or chargeable to different clients. In your case the exercise will confirm or clarify the accuracy of your estimates as to where you thought your time went. It will also give a clearer indication of how much time you are actually spending on various issues and give you food for thought about the value of each in terms of helping pupils learn. And of course it will also indicate where you might be wasting time, and the rest of this book is devoted to identifying the timewasters within your day and how to deal with them.

You may want to focus on time wasted during the teaching day and keep an accurate time-log of some of your lessons. The format is similar but you will want to note the activities every five minutes instead of each 15. The log would look like this.

Time-log for a lesson

Time	Activity	Time	Activity
5 mins		10 mins	
15 mins		20 mins	
25 mins		30 mins	
35 mins		40 mins	
45 mins		50 mins	
55 mins		60 mins	

Activities

Time spent on each

getting started
giving out materials/books
giving instructions
teaching
keeping order
marking
assessing pupil progress
checking understanding of
    learning
    instructions
collecting work in
dismissing class

The most accurate way of keeping this log is to have some-one else do it for you. You may be able to set up paired observation schemes where a partner keeps your lesson time-log for you and you return the favour. This will mean an investment in terms of non-contact time, the supply budget, or getting senior staff to cover classes in their non-contact time. You could always consider an education-industry link up with an outsider observing you at work for the day and keeping the log for you. Another possibility is to link up with your local teacher training establishment to develop a scheme where students workshadow you for a day or so and keep a time-log as part of the process. You could also use the time you gain from having students on teaching practice in school to enable staff to monitor each other's use of time. In some schools the pupils have kept such logs on their teachers. What better way of improving your teaching than by having direct feedback from your pupils? There are many excuses for not keeping an accurate time-log but there are equally many opportunities for keeping them accurately and assessing exactly where your time is going. If you can involve pupils, parents, governors and the local business community, you will be raising the awareness of those groups about the pressure on your time, and gaining some important allies in your claim for more adequate funding to enable the school to provide even better quality education. They will see at first hand how time constraints are affecting the quality of the teaching as well as being confronted with the accurate statistical evidence they themselves have collected! They will also appreciate how serious you are in your intentions to improve your time-management skills.

CHAPTER 3
Identifying Timewasters

Having done a comprehensive audit of where your time actually does go, you can begin to identify the major timewasters and ways to tackle them. In most cases the major timewasters fall in to a small range of categories which are:

- poor planning
- poor organization
- paperwork
- meetings
- interruptions.

Go through your time-logs and identify the timewasters, those activities which are not productive, and list them against the categories above. For example, under 'poor planning' you may include things like:

- not having enough materials prepared for a particular lesson
- not having everything you need to be able to complete a particular task
- having to queue up for the photocopier because everyone else wants it at the same time
- underestimating how long a job will take
- finding everything needs doing at once
- having to concentrate on very important tasks when you feel worn out
- and so on.

Under 'poor organization' you may have issues like:

- looking for papers, documents, etc.
- not having tools and materials accessible
- not having tools and materials well labelled
- not having equipment well organized
- having no recognized system for giving out equipment and materials
- having to spend too much time tidying up after lessons
- having an untidy stock cupboard and book shelves
- and so on.

Under 'paperwork' your timewasters may include things like:

- looking for papers you need
- the relevance of the paperwork to your objectives
- the lack of usefulness of some paperwork
- a poor filing system
- the amount of paperwork
- having paperwork given to you which is not relevant
- having no system for dealing with paperwork
- having papers spread all over your desk
- not prioritizing your paperwork
- and so on.

Meetings are often cited as a major timewaster and some of the reasons you have identified may include:

- meetings which don't achieve anything
- not knowing what the meeting is about beforehand
- people being poorly prepared
- poor chairing of meetings
- meetings being dominated by a few people
- too few people contributing to the meeting
- meetings not being focused enough
- meetings not starting on time
- meetings over-running
- meetings for the sake of having meetings
- and so on.

Interruptions are often a major source of wasted time. Look through your time-log and identify how often these have caused you to stop what you were doing to deal with something else. These might include:

- colleagues who want a word
- pupils who need to see you
- a distraught parent
- a senior member of staff who wants to see you
- a visiting inspector/adviser who has just popped in
- a governor visiting the school
- and so on.

We will spend some time looking at each of these areas throughout the rest of this book and considering some of the strategies that you might try to remedy them. Some of the ideas you will be able to implement yourself while others may require you to negotiate agreed systems with colleagues within and beyond the school.

You may at this stage want to carry on through this book as it is written or you may have identified particular areas of concern, in which case you may want to read those chapters first. To help you to decide which chapters you need most, try listing your major timewasters on the following chart.

Assessing time management priorities

Category/ Timewaster	Planning	Organization	Paper-work	Meetings	Interruptions

CHAPTER 4
Planning

Effective planning is essential to good time management.

It can be broken down into long-, medium- and short-term planning. We will look at each in turn and see the impact of effective planning on your daily routines.

Long-term planning

Before the start of a new academic year you will have made plans for things you want to achieve before the end of that year. These will largely derive from the school development plan. These plans will have dates attached to them for their completion and you can put these into your diary before the new year starts. You can also write in fixed dates like parents' evenings, sports days, exams etc, as these have a direct impact on your short-term planning.

Having put these dates in your diary you can then work backwards from them and put in important interim dates. For example, if parents' evening is on June 20 then:

- reports need to written by the end of May, which means
- any assessments to be included in the reports need to be completed by the middle of May, which means
- they need to be written and prepared by mid April, which means
- completing the class work by the end of April.

A useful technique for planning in the long term is to list all the tasks that have to be accomplished to achieve the long-term goal. Try to get them in the order in which they have to occur, bearing in mind that some will be concurrent. Write them on a grid so that you can see the deadline for each aspect. For example, if you have to put on the end of year play you will have a list that looks like this:

TIME PLAN FOR THE END OF YEAR PLAY

Tasks	Wk1	Wk2	Wk3	Wk4	Wk5	Wk6	Wk7	etc
Write script	■	■						
Have it typed		■	■					
Have it copied		■						
Book hall	■							
Inform parents		■						
Audition				■				
Make costumes								
Make props								
Design set								
Make set								
Rehearse actors								
Recruit backstage								
Rehearse backstage								
Get make up								
Rehearse make up								
Print tickets								
etc.								

Having listed all the tasks, go through your grid and block in the box when that particular task needs to be done. The example has been started for you. See if you can finish it. This ensures that you can keep track of the progress of the particular project and make sure it sticks to target, or adjust the dates, including completion date, to be more realistic if you find all the tasks do not fit into the time you have allowed. Try doing this exercise for one of your long-term projects, like rewriting a policy document which would include tasks like:

- reviewing the existing policy
- checking current legislation
- researching ideas
- attending in-service courses
- consulting colleagues
- etc.

There is a grid below for you to use. It covers a year, with a box for each month. Once you have completed it with the months shaded for the completion of each task, you can transfer the information to termly grids divided into weeks so that you can be more precise in your targeting of completion dates, or you could use a year planner and be more precise, down to actual dates for completion.

PLANNING GRID FOR A LONG TERM PROJECT

Project _____

Tasks/months	1	2	3	4	5	6	7	8	9	10	11	12

Medium-term planning

Having set the long-term plan you need now to transfer the tasks to a medium-term plan. The natural timescale for this would be a single term. In transferring the tasks from your long-term plan to your termly one you can be aware of the times of term which are busy enough without adding in extra work. It does help to focus the mind and keep you to your timescale. Take the project you have just planned over a full year and allocate the tasks from the early part of it to specific weeks of the first term using the following grid.

MEDIUM-TERM PLANNING GRID

Project _____

_____ **term**

Tasks/weeks	1	2	3	4	5	6	7	8	9	10	11	12

If you can produce your long- and medium-term grids on acetates (and persuade your colleagues to do likewise) you can overlay them to see if there are any major clashes which will produce undue pressure on each other or on central services like typing or reprographics. If this is done at an early stage in long-term planning you can avoid potential disasters, such as someone else having booked the photocopier when you desperately need it.

You can now begin to relate your long-term planning to your daily diary and 'to do' list. Having allocated tasks from a specific long-term project to actual weeks of the term, you have to find the times within each week to complete the tasks allocated to that week. This is where you move into short-term planning.

Short-term planning

One of the most fundamental mistakes people make in short-term planning is to plan only for what they perceive as the important tasks. For example, people will make a note in their diaries of meetings they have to attend but they rarely make a note in their diary that they are going to spend an hour marking books or preparing work, or working on the kind of tasks they have identified as necessary for completion of a long-term project. Teachers will plan effectively for lessons to ensure that they know when they are teaching what to whom and that they have all the necessary equipment and materials for the lesson. How often do they similarly plan for mounting, marking, report writing, etc.?

You must begin therefore by listing all the tasks for the week, however routine and mundane they may seem. Then you can block in those where the times are beyond your control, like your class teaching commitment and meetings you have to attend. This leaves you with blocks of time over which you can have some control, so allocate blocks to the other tasks and *write them into your diary or planner.*

This immediately elevates the status of those tasks which have been denied a diary space previously and also acts as a powerful reminder of how little time you have. As long as you have some spaces in your diary it looks as though you have time in hand. So start now by listing the tasks for next week under two headings: *must do* and *would like to do*. Include the normal everyday routine things *and* the tasks you need to complete to keep your long-term projects on target. Include what the job is, the target for completing it and how long you think you need to do it. Also include what you need to accomplish the task in the same way that you note what you need for a particular lesson when planning your teaching. The headings below will help you. Building in what you need to accomplish your tasks should help to avoid everyone arriving at the photocopier at the same time!

Must do

What	*By when*	*Time needed*	*Things needed*

Would like to do

What	*By when*	*Time needed*	*Things needed*

You then need to transfer the tasks you have identified to spaces in your diary or planner so that as many tasks as possible are allocated spaces. If you have major tasks left over without a space, you have a couple of choices. First, you might re-think your priorities to see if some tasks could be swapped. Second, you can go to your boss and seek her/his advice on how to fit all the tasks you've got into the time available. If you have a genuine grievance about a lack of time, your boss will be able to see it from your planner. A simple format is to have a page a day broken into hour or half-hour slots. A completed daily plan might look like this:

Daily plan (Example)
Date February 28

7.00		7.30	leave for school
8.00	preparing lessons	8.30	photocopying
9.00	teaching	9.30	teaching
10.00	teaching	10.30	playground duty
11.00	teaching	11.30	teaching
12.00	lunch	12.30	preparing lessons
1.00	teaching	1.30	teaching
2.00	teaching	2.30	coffee break, see...about...
3.00	teaching	3.30	see parent
4.00	mounting work	4.30	marking books
5.00	checking catalogues	5.30	writing out order
6.00	leave for home	6.30	eating!
7.00	leave for school	7.30	parents' meeting
8.00	parents' meeting	8.30	parents' meeting
9.00	leave for home	9.30	reading *TES*

Now try completing your own plan for tomorrow. Try building in contingency time to cope with the inevitable emergency.

Daily plan

Date _____

7.00	7.30
8.00	8.30
9.00	9.30
10.00	10.30
11.00	11.30
12.00	12.30
1.00	1.30
2.00	2.30
3.00	3.30
4.00	4.30
5.00	5.30
6.00	6.30
7.00	7.30
8.00	8.30
9.00	9.30

The effectiveness of your planning will depend to an extent on whether you can do your tasks without interruption in the times you have allocated, and we will address that issue later in the chapter. It will also depend on whether you have allocated the tasks to the most appropriate times.

As a general rule you should timetable important tasks requiring a lot of concentration to the times of the day when you are most alert – your prime time. As this is usually in the morning it might be worth considering timetabling these tasks to the hour before school begins, rather than at 4pm when you have just dismissed your class and are tired. You also need to schedule the tasks requiring most concentration to the times when you are least likely to be interrupted by either pupils or colleagues, so getting to school half an hour earlier in the morning can pay dividends if it allows you uninterrupted prime time on important tasks.

When prioritizing tasks, place them in the context of helping pupils to learn. Given the choice of two tasks for one space, choose the one which will have the greatest impact on children's learning. This is rather like the sales person choosing between two customers for the final appointment of the day: the obvious choice is the one who is likely to give the biggest order. Which of your tasks will have the greatest impact on your pupils' learning?

Prioritizing tasks

Try putting this list of tasks in priority order. At the top of the list will be the task that you think will have the greatest impact upon children's learning and standards of achievement:

- marking books
- tidying the classroom
- preparing worksheets
- mounting children's work

- attending a routine staff meeting
- reading the *Times Educational Supplement*
- attending a course on an area in which you are not confident
- sharpening pencils
- listening to a sales rep's presentation on a new maths scheme
- planning assessment sheets
- writing a new scheme of work based on the latest National Curriculum orders
- running a staff workshop on a specified curriculum area
- visiting a museum to which you are to take children next week
- planning next term's work with colleagues.

The order you decide upon will depend very much on your own particular situation. The important thing is to realize that some tasks have a greater impact on children's learning than others, and these are the ones that should take priority. Convincing your boss of this may be another matter, of course!

Prime time

Take the same list of tasks that you have just put in priority order and, bearing in mind when your own prime time is, allocate them to specific times of day so that you tackle the important ones when you are most able to cope with them and the least important ones at those times when you really don't function at all well. Arrange them in the following table.

MATCHING TASKS TO TIMES

Tasks/times	Before school	Lunch time	After school	Evening

Urgent or important

In planning your use of time and allocating tasks to times, you need to remember the difference between urgent tasks and important ones. Urgent tasks need doing quickly but don't necessarily take a long time to complete. Important tasks often take some concentrated effort to complete and do require time. Some tasks of course will be urgent *and* important and they require a lot of time now. Others will be neither urgent nor important, in which case you should be asking yourself why you are doing them at all. Bear in mind that your perspective on these matters may not coincide with that of others!

Take the following list of tasks that might require doing in a day and decide which are urgent, which are important, and which are both. Tick the column where you would put each task.

Urgent or important tasks

Task	urgent	important	both	neither
Seeing an anxious parent				
Attending to a broken window				
Seeing a school adviser				
Mounting work				
Planning next term				
Dealing with a fight				
An appraisal interview				
Meeting an OFSTED inspector				
Completing records				
A case conference				
Writing curriculum policy				

Important tasks generally need time, and preferably prime time, allocated to them. Urgent tasks need attending to immediately. Too often we confuse the two and talk about an urgent meeting with a school adviser or inspector when what we really mean is a potentially important meeting.

If teachers planned for their non-teaching time as effectively as they do for their teaching time, there would be little call for time management for teachers. Try it and see!

CHAPTER 5
Organization

organisatin paragraph.

Poor organization can waste a lot of time both within the classroom and beyond. In this section we will look at ways of improving classroom organization and the organization of administrative duties beyond the teaching day to use your limited time more effectively.

Classroom organization

When we looked at your current use of time, we identified a range of classroom tasks and you estimated how long you spent on each in a week, and then kept a time-log for some lessons to check the accuracy of your assumptions. If we can save a few minutes from each lesson on each item then the total saving could add up to a substantial amount of extra teaching time. Some aspects will lend themselves to greater savings than others of course, but let us work down the list in the order it appears in the earlier section.

Getting started

Getting started includes pupils arriving for the lesson, entering the classroom, getting themselves organized in their seats and getting out what they need for the lesson. To see whether you have any major problems here, try the following short self-assessment exercise. It breaks down the beginning of the lesson into various aspects where time may be lost.

Do your pupils	mostly	often	sometimes	rarely
Arrive on time for lessons?				
Go straight to their own places?				
Have whatever they need?				
Get out whatever they need?				
Sit quietly waiting instructions?				
Get straight on with their work?				

If you have ticked the *mostly* column for each aspect, you should be wasting very little time at the beginnings of lessons because you are well-organized and your pupils know what you expect. If you have ticks in other columns, you need to look at the routines you have in place (if any) for the start of lessons and ensure that your pupils know what they are and adhere to them.

Teaching

To ensure that your teaching is making the most effective use of the time available, you need to make sure it is effectively planned to be accessible to all of your pupils. Everyone has a preferred learning style out of the four which have been identified as:

- activist
- pragmatist
- reflector
- theorist.

This means considering each individual's preferred learning style and ensuring that you present your teaching in such a way as to encompass each of the learning styles. The characteristics of each style are as follows.

Activist

These learners become fully involved in new experiences, living for the here and now and ready to try anything once.

Pragmatist

These learners like to try things to see if they work in practice. They want to test new ideas in practical situations, and work on the basis that if it works it must be good.

Reflector

The reflector stands back from the action to observe from a variety of angles, taking time to reflect before reaching any conclusions.

Theorist

Theorists prefer a logical structured approach, developing sound and sometimes complex theories from what they observe and prefer objective rather than subjective judgements.

You will have a preferred learning style and tend to teach the way you prefer to learn. This may mean less effective learning for three-quarters of your class who may well have a different preferred learning style. Try listing your classes (or one of them) and ticking which learning style you think each pupil prefers. In a future lesson look for evidence to check your assumptions.

PREFERRED LEARNING STYLES OF PUPILS

Pupil	Activist	Pragmatist	Reflector	Theorist

The more often you can present your teaching in each of the four styles the more likelihood there is of all the class being able to understand the points you are making, leading to less frustration all round. The usual problem is that the teacher explains in her or his preferred learning style and then simply repeats that explanation when faced with pupils who do not grasp the ideas.

Well-organized teaching also means:

- having very clear objectives
- knowing what you will do
- knowing what the learners will do
- having the appropriate resources to hand
- knowing how long each part of the lesson will take.

A simple grid with five columns like the one below can provide a useful check that you are well organized.

LESSON PLANNING

Objectives	What I will do	What the learners will do	Resources	Time

Giving out books and collecting them back

If your time-log showed that you spend time at the start of each lesson giving out books and materials, you should consider the delegation of such routine tasks to your pupils. Delegation is one of the least used but most effective time-management tools. As a teacher you are fairly constrained in who you can delegate to, but you should take the opportunities to encourage your pupils to accept some responsibility for some of the more routine classroom tasks. Delegation is simply giving someone else the authority to do part of your job. There are two reasons for delegating:

● it reduces your workload, thereby saving you time
● it develops the people you delegate to.

Clearly, delegating routine tasks like giving out books and materials will achieve both of these things.

In order to delegate effectively, however, you have to train those to whom you are delegating. Having explained and shown them exactly what they are to do and how they are to do it, you need to provide enough support to ensure that they cope successfully and to offer praise and encouragement, especially early on when they might make mistakes. Remember also that you can delegate the responsibility for such routine tasks but you retain the accountability. If the job is done incorrectly it may be due to your poor training or lack of supervision rather than their lack of commitment or understanding.

There will not be many jobs that you can delegate but it might be worth looking methodically at some of them to identify what you could pass on. Try completing the following table to see just how many routine tasks you do at the moment which could be usefully delegated.

DELEGATION

What I do now	
What I could delegate	
Who I could delegate it to	
Why I should delegate it to her/him	

Clearing up at the end of lessons

If you are having to spend time tidying the classroom at the end of lessons you have clearly not developed your delegation skills adequately yet! Ensure that in organizing your teaching you allow enough time for pupils to return everything to its proper place, leaving the classroom ready for the next lesson.

Giving instructions

This can sometimes be a time-consuming business because pupils need to have instructions given several times over before they understand the task. The lack of understanding may be due to their inability to listen, but it could also be due to your instructions: you need to make them as clear as you can the first time. Recent research has shown that everyone has a dominant sensory system giving a preference to communicate using terms which are visual, or auditory or kinaesthetic. If you have a preference for the *visual* you will use terms such as:

- 'Do you see what I'm saying?'
- 'That looks right.'
- 'What is your view?'

A preference for the *auditory* will result in you using terms such as:

- 'That rings a bell.'
- 'Does that sound okay?'
- 'Listen.'
- 'I hear what you're saying'

A preference for the *kinaesthetic* will result in you using terms such as:

- 'How does that strike you?'
- 'That doesn't feel right.'
- 'Could you handle that?'

In giving instructions you will use the language of your preferred sensory system which will be shared by only some of the class. To ensure that everyone has equal access to the instructions, you need to use terminology that is visual, auditory and kinaesthetic. This should save you from some of the repetition of instructions.

Try listening to some of your class and picking out the words and phrases they use which indicate their natural sensory preference. Use a chart like the one below to log a whole class to appreciate the range of preferences.

SENSORY PREFERENCES OF PUPILS

Pupil	Visual	Auditory	Kinaesthetic

You also need to ensure that the whole class can see you when giving instructions, as the majority of any face-to-face communication is non-verbal. The estimates vary, but some researchers believe that the message is transmitted in the following proportions:

- 6 per cent through the words
- 14 per cent through the tone of voice
- 80 per cent through the body language.

Clearly if some of your class cannot see you when you are telling them what to do, they are distinctly disadvantaged.

Keeping order

If you are finding that too much time is being wasted just maintaining order in the classroom and keeping pupils on task it might be worth assessing why this is. Try logging who is off task and what might be the cause. Once you have some firm ideas of what is causing pupils to be off task you can begin to address those particular problems which may be covered elsewhere in this section. Focus initially on no more than six pupils using the grid below.

LOGGING-OFF TASK PUPILS

Pupil	1	2	3	4	5	6
Waiting for instructions						
Waiting for more work						
Waiting for marking						
Waiting for resources						
Waiting for help						
Looking for things						
Disturbed by other pupils' work						
etc						

If you find a pattern emerging, you need to look at how your classroom organization may be contributing to the problem. If pupils are off task because they are waiting for things, for instance, you need to look at ways of organizing your classroom and lessons so that pupils can become more independent.

Consider ways in which you organize your classroom resources so that pupils can access them without having to wait each time they need something. Train them to get what they need sensibly and safely and return it properly afterwards. This will take time initially but repay itself as the term progresses. Ensure that there is plenty of meaningful work for the early finishers to get on with and that the work is well matched to abilities through effective differentiation (one of the things OFSTED inspectors will be looking for). It is easy to blame off-task pupils on everyone and everything else but, before you do so, analyse your own classroom organization to see how it may be preventing your pupils from working effectively and causing you time-management problems.

Marking work and assessing pupil performance

Work has to be marked and you cannot avoid spending some time doing it. Make sure it is meaningful, however, and that it influences future planning. As far as possible mark with the pupil present so that you can give feedback straight away. Consider ways that older pupils could be involved in self-marking of routine work where there are answer books, with you checking their marking. Have an effective system for checking that marking is up to date. A simple class list that is ticked as each piece is marked can quickly show you any gaps.

Complete assessment records systematically as they are marked so that the work does not mount up for the end of term. Have the necessary record books handy so that you can record marks almost as you mark the work.

Checking understanding

You need to check that pupils have understood what you have been trying to teach them. Try to build in to your lessons opportunities for pupils to demonstrate their learning in an easily recognizable way which will not require an extensive use of your time. Can you include a practical task of some sort which will not only test their understanding but encourage them to see the practical implications of it? Try to ensure that assessment tasks are, as far as possible, also developing or reinforcing learning.

Having looked at the impact of classroom organisation on your time management, try the test below to see how effective you are.

Assessing the effectiveness of classroom organization

	Yes	No
Pupils settle quickly on arriving		
They have what they need		
They soon get out what they need		
They know where resources are kept		
They access resources sensibly/safely		
They return resources to their places		
They help to give out books, etc		
They never queue at your desk		
They know where to put finished work		
They sometimes mark their own work		
They record work completed for you		
They nearly always work on task		
They understand instructions first time		
They rarely ask for help		
They tidy up before leaving.		

The more ticks you got in the 'yes' column the better:

15 means that you are perfectly organized in the classroom.

10–15 means that your classroom organization is very good.

5–10 means that you need to improve some areas of classroom organization.

0–5 means you are wasting a lot of your time and that of your pupils.

Organizing non-teaching tasks

When you are organizing your non-teaching tasks, there are a few fairly simple rules to remember.

Do one job at a time

To try to do several tasks at once will result in several half-done tasks. Decide which you are going to do and work at it until it is as complete as it can be. Clear it away before starting on the next one.

Have a clear desk

Have on your desk only what you need for the task in hand. If your planning has been effective you should have gathered everything you need in advance. Have only those things relevant to the job so that you are not distracted by other bits and pieces.

Avoid interruptions

There will be times when you need to concentrate on an important task and interruptions will break that concentration and waste valuable time. Try agreeing a system with colleagues for keeping certain times of each week free for concentrated work when no one will interrupt anyone else; you can have other times for tasks requiring less concentration when colleagues are allowed to pop in. Everyone will benefit.

Organize your workspace

Make sure your desk and your office, if you have one, are tidy. Everything should have its place, just as in the classroom, so that you do not spend time searching for things that you need. A simple way of checking whether your workspace is as organized as it should be is to try to explain to someone else where to find something. If your colleague can go straight to it, you are well-organized. If they can't, or worse still you cannot tell them, then you need to do some tidying urgently!

Organize your paperwork

The next section outlines strategies for coping with the paperwork which has become an increasing burden for teachers lately.

CHAPTER 6
Paperwork

There is a great emphasis these days on the amount of paperwork that teachers have to do. There are claims that the sheer volume of paperwork is detracting from the primary function of teaching children. Consequently, there is a greater need than ever for teachers to organize their management of paperwork more effectively. In this matter they have the same difficulties as most professional people, and similar strategies to those used in any effective office will help.

The first thing to consider is the range of options with paperwork. Basically there are only four possible things to do:

- act on it
- pass it on
- file it
- bin it.

While you might like to take the final action with most of your paperwork, the demands of the job are such that inevitably there will be some administration. However, too often we spend time shuffling papers round the desk rather than tackling them, and this wastes a great deal of time. It has been suggested that on average we spend 22 minutes a day just looking for papers that we need, and that every piece of paper on your desk will distract you up to five times a day. A more systematic approach can save you valuable time.

As well as having to deal with paperwork generated by other people you may well find that you too are generating paperwork. In this case you need to ask yourself each time you are tempted to produce another piece of paper for circulation what impact it will have on the standards of achievement and quality of learning of the pupils. Then you need to consider whether the impact it will have will be greater than leaving colleagues with the time they will take on your piece of paper to plan their teaching, mark books or whatever. If you decide that the impact of your piece of paper in this context is not going to enhance standards of achievement and quality of learning you need to seriously question the value of the piece of paper.

Handling incoming paperwork

Bearing in mind that there are only four possibilities with each item of paperwork that arrives on your desk, the first task is to sort it accordingly into the four piles. Try listing your paperwork for this week under the four headings depending whether it requires you to do something, is for information, is on the wrong desk or is irrelevant. Use the table on the opposite page to enter all the incoming papers under the most appropriate column.

Having gone through the exercise, you will need to tackle the actual paperwork as it arises. Given that there are only four choices, let us look at each in turn.

SORTING INCOMING PAPERS

Paper	Act on	Pass on	File	Bin

Act on it

If a piece of incoming paperwork demands some action on your part, deal with it straight away whenever possible. To see how many times you handle each piece of paper, put a red dot on each paper each time you pick it up. The more dots, the more time wasted shuffling papers rather than dealing with them.

If the paper requires more time and attention than you can give it now, there are three steps in dealing with it:

1. Make a note on your 'to do' list of when you will deal with it. If you have organized your planning effectively you will be able to allocate the paper to a specific time and date in your planner.
2. File the paper under the most appropriate heading in your well-organized filing system.
3. Retrieve it at the time and date allocated to it and work on it.

Under no circumstances should you leave papers on your desk to remind you to do them later, as they will only distract you from your existing work. Have on your desk only what you need for the current task and nothing else. If you have an in-tray, make sure it is placed behind you or in a cupboard out of sight somewhere. This should prevent you from shuffling through looking for something easier to do when the going gets tough on the current task.

Passing it on

Some of the papers landing on your desk should not be there in the first place. This may be because:

- you are not the most appropriate person to deal with it
- someone else has dumped their problem on to you
- you should delegate it to someone else
- it is circulating the entire staff for information
- it has arrived on your desk by mistake.

Whatever the reason for it being there, make sure it leaves for the most appropriate destination as soon as possible.

Filing it

In order to keep your desk completely free of everything except the papers you are actually working on at the moment, you need an efficient filing system. If you have confidence in your system, you are more likely to use it effectively, so spend some time ensuring that you have a system that works. Review the actual system occasionally to check that it is still coping with the demands you are making of it.

Before you file anything you need to ask, why do I need to keep this paper? Refer back to your list of paperwork and the four headings you placed each item under. Take all the filing items and put them in the following chart. Then write alongside each the reason you need to file it at all.

REASONS FOR FILING PAPERS

Paper	Reasons for filing it

Having decided that you have valid reasons for filing some of your papers, the second question is, how long do I need to keep each paper?

Filing cabinets have a tendency to swallow huge amounts of paper which never see the light of day again. This makes finding the bit you desperately need a very time-consuming business as you unearth mountains of out-of-date memos and minutes that you filed because you could not think of anything else to do with them. Before filing anything, decide how long you need to keep it for and put a date on it when you will review whether to keep it or not. Set time aside regularly to review the contents of your filing system so that you systematically keep only what needs to be kept, and save some of the time you waste searching through papers that should not even be there.

Refer back to your list of papers you considered filing. Put those that you decided were worth filing into the chart below and put alongside each the date when you will review whether to keep them or not.

REVIEWING FILING

Paper	Date to be reviewed

Binning it

We are often tempted to file papers that should really go in the bin; teachers are notorious for hoarding things. Examples include reports that might be useful one day, catalogues from suppliers that might come in handy sometime, and all sorts of other unsolicited mail. Try following the rule, 'if in doubt, sling it out'. You can bet that if you find you do need whatever it is in the future, someone nearby will have kept a copy or you will be able to get another from the original source. It is sometimes more efficient to keep the address of the catalogue company in your address book and request a catalogue when you need one, rather than keeping the catalogue you are hardly going to use cluttering up your desk.

CHAPTER 7
Meetings

Meetings take up an enormous amount of time for most professional people; teachers are no exception. A survey of executives showed that around 70 per cent of them felt that meetings were a waste of time and that around 70 per cent of them had had no training in meetings skills. Teachers would probably produce similar results if they were surveyed. Meetings can become an incredible drain on your already inadequate supply of time without necessarily producing a worthwhile return on your investment. In commercial terms, every minute the salesperson is not selling, because they are in a meeting of some sort, is potentially lost revenue to the company. In teaching, every minute spent in an unproductive meeting is potentially an opportunity lost to do something to enhance the standards of learning of your pupils. Consequently, you should judge the value of projected meetings by the impact they are likely to have on standards within your classroom. That is not to say that we do not need meetings in education; they are an important part of working life. What we do need is to ensure that meetings actually achieve what they set out to achieve and that they do something to help pupils to learn.

A good starting point is to list all the work meetings you attend, including:

- staff meetings
- parents' meetings

- moderating meetings
- year group/department meetings
- cross-phase meetings
- governors' meetings
- meetings with outside agencies
- planning meetings
- and so on.

Complete the following table with all the work meetings you attend.

MEETINGS ATTENDED

Meeting	Frequency	Length

Once you have completed your list, check against your time-logs and see if the length of the meetings in your list corresponds to the actual time spent on them. Then work out how long you spend in total on meetings over an average week, month, term and year. Using the salary table given earlier, you can work out how much it costs for you to attend these meetings. For example, if you attend an hour-long staff meeting every week, it is easy enough to work out the cost of your attendance at that meeting over the year. If you save some of the time spent on meetings by either dispensing with some of them or by running them more efficiently, you will gain some much-needed time for other tasks.

J K Galbraith once said:

Meetings are indispensable when you don't want to do something.

We have meetings for a whole range of reasons, but sometimes they are not very obvious. Go through your list of work meetings again, but this time put in the reason why you think they are held. If possible, get some of your colleagues to write down what they think the purposes of these meetings are and compare notes to see how clear the purposes really are. If there is a range of widely different perceived purposes, you are probably wasting some valuable time because people are not clear why they are there and therefore won't contribute as effectively as they might.

Reasons for meetings

Meeting	Purpose

To be effective, meetings need to have clear objectives which are understood and accepted by all those in attendance. If there is confusion about the objectives of the meeting and its basic purpose, this is likely to render it less effective than it might be. So, if you are convening a meeting, do seriously consider the purpose before you rush to invite people to commit some of their valuable time. Ask yourself what the participants will have gained from attending.

Having asked that question, go on to ask whether what they will gain is worth the investment or whether they might gain more from having that time to do other things. Similarly, before accepting invitations to meetings, ask what benefits your pupils will get from your attendance and whether these outweigh the benefits they might get from your not attending and doing something else instead.

Take your list of work meetings and put them in the table below. Then give each a score on the scale according to the benefits they bring to your pupils' learning. The higher the score the greater the benefits. Be prepared to justify your scoring by producing evidence of the benefits!

BENEFITS OF MEETINGS TO PUPILS

Meeting	0	1	2	3	4	5	6

Having allocated your meetings a score according to the benefits they bring to pupils' learning, you can now compare the amount of time you spend on each meeting in a year with the potential benefits it brings. As many meetings in many organizations are held out of habit, this can be an unnerving exercise!

Any meetings which failed to score on the last exercise need serious consideration with colleagues to assess whether they failed to score because they genuinely do not bring benefits to pupils' learning or because you cannot appreciate their impact.

You also need to compare the length of time each type of meeting takes over the school year with the perceived benefits to pupils' learning. Clearly if you are spending far more time on routine administration which does little to help pupils to learn than on, say, planning lessons, you need to consider faster ways of doing the administration or even whether it needs doing at all.

Having completed the exercises so far will have given you an insight into how many of your meetings are worthwhile and how many you might need to reassess. What you need to consider now is how to make the essential meetings more effective so that they produce maximum benefits in the shortest time.

Organizing effective meetings

Given that so many people consider so many meetings to be less than useful and that so few people have ever had any training in organizing them, it is hardly surprising that they rank high up in the list of major timewasters. To be effective in organizing meetings we can begin by looking at why so many of them fail. All of us have experienced the disastrous meeting when we wondered why on earth we ever agreed to turn up. Think back to some of the worst meetings you have attended and try listing half a dozen reasons why meetings fail. We will then look at how to ensure that meetings are an effective use of time and produce worthwhile results.

Why meetings fail

1.

2.

3.

4.

5.

6.

You might have included some of the following:

- Lack of a clear purpose – the objectives of the meeting have not been clearly thought through or conveyed to those in attendance.
- Poor planning – there is insufficient notice of the meeting, the agenda is poorly planned or non-existent, and little thought has gone into the choice of venue, participants, etc.
- Poor control – the chairperson fails to keep the meeting on target, or goes to the other extreme where no one is allowed to participate.
- Poor communication before, during or after the meeting, which leads to confusion and frustration.
- Indecisiveness –
  - long drawn out discussions are mistaken for decision making

- the meeting lacks the courage to make a decision
- decisions are influenced by hidden agendas.

● Unclear outcomes – no one is quite sure what has been decided and who should be doing what by when.

Planning a meeting

To avoid the pitfalls of failed meetings requires effective planning. The first stage in organizing an effective meeting is to set clear objectives. If you can set them in terms of what will have been achieved by the meeting, they should be clear. For example:

by the end of this meeting we will have agreed the dates for parents' evenings

is more likely to produce a successful outcome than,

we will have a meeting about parents' evenings.

Similarly, a meeting to

devise and agree a whole-school marking policy

is more likely to produce results than

a meeting about marking

although you are likely to need more than one in this case!

Look back to three or four recent meetings that you attended and see whether you can be sure what the objectives were. These might be meetings you convened or ones that you attended. Try comparing what you thought the objectives were with what colleagues (especially the convener) thought they were. Complete the following table.

OBJECTIVES FOR RECENT MEETINGS

Meeting	Objectives
1.	
2.	
3.	
4.	

Clearly, if you know what the objectives were, you can assess how effective the meetings were. Try now going back over the list and awarding marks out of ten for how effectively each meeting achieved its objectives as you perceived them. Meetings that do not go a long way towards meeting their objectives are wasting valuable time which could be used for more important things.

Having looked back to assess the effectiveness and clarity of the objectives for some recent meetings, try now looking forward to three or four meetings that you have to organize and see if you have set clear objectives in terms of what they will achieve. List them below.

OBJECTIVES FOR FORTHCOMING MEETINGS

Meeting	Objectives
1.	
2.	
3.	
4.	

Assessing the need for a meeting

Having set the objectives that you hope to achieve through your meetings, try asking how you could achieve them other than by holding a meeting. At this stage you can be as outrageous as you want to be – hang the potential expense because all you are doing is brainstorming possibilities. Write down the first ideas that come into your head, however ludicrous they turn out to be, in case some of them turn out not to be so daft after all. Don't attempt to place a valuc on them at this stage. You might include things like:

- sending a memo
- telephoning everyone
- going to see everyone individually
- etc.

ALTERNATIVE WAYS OF ACHIEVING THE OBJECTIVES
OF A MEETING

1.
2.
3.
4.
5.
6.
7.
8.
9.
10.
11.
12.
13.
14.
15.

The next step is to consider whether any of the ideas on your list would achieve your objectives as effectively as a meeting. Begin by crossing out all the ideas which are obviously less effective, less efficient or both. Video-conferencing might be a realistic alternative for a multinational with offices all over the world, but is not likely to be a viable alternative in your school.

Having deleted all the obviously less effective and efficient alternatives, if you have any ideas left you need to consider them before you convene your meeting. How likely you are to find a realistic alternative depends largely upon the type of meeting you are thinking of calling. Meetings generally fall into a small range of types, including:

- *information exchanges,* as in a parents' meeting where teachers and parents share information about the pupils
- *presentations,* as in a new parents' induction meeting where parents attend to seek information about the school
- *progress reviews,* as in meetings to check the progress of policy documents

- *planning meetings*, as in planning lessons or schemes of work
- *discussions*, as in initial discussions on the budget, staff training needs, etc.
- *decision-making meetings*, as in making decisions on budget allocations and other policy issues
- *team building*, as in a department working on a common project partly with the aim of developing effective team working for future projects
- *negotiations*, as in departments or curriculum leaders negotiating for their share of the overall budget.

Some meetings will encompass more than one of these, of course. The important thing is to avoid calling a very expensive and time-consuming meeting unless there is a real benefit to be gained by doing so.

Who should attend your meeting?

Many teachers will have attended meetings and come away wondering why they were ever invited. When convening meetings you need to consider who to invite and why. As a rule, people need to be there for some of the following reasons:

- they have information to give
- they need to receive information from the meeting
- they have expertise the meeting will need
- they have particular responsibility for the meeting or issues within it
- they are annoyed and need an opportunity to air grievances and be consulted.

Look at some of your recent meetings and draw up a list of those who attended. Alongside each name write the reason or reasons for that person attending.

You may well find that people need not attend every meeting of a particular group, but only certain ones where they will offer or gain something from being there. Equally, it may

ATTENDANCE AT MEETINGS

Attendee	Reason for attending

be that people do not need to attend all of each meeting, but would be better off attending only for the sections that are relevant to them. If you are arranging meetings, let people know whether they are required for the whole meeting or for only part of it. Similarly if you are invited to a meeting and from the agenda it looks as though you will not gain a lot from it, ask if you may attend just the relevant part.

The agenda

Every meeting has an agenda but not every meeting has a published one. Usually the chairperson knows the agenda and in the best meetings everyone else is familiar with it too. In this way everyone can prepare effectively and the meeting can be conducted efficiently. The benefits of a published agenda also include:

- letting people know how long it will last
- whether they need to be there or not
- whether they need to attend for the whole meeting or not

- what preparation they need to do before the meeting.

In order to achieve those benefits, the agenda needs to contain the right information. Try drawing up a list of the information you think a meeting agenda should contain.

CONTENTS OF AN EFFECTIVE AGENDA

1.
2.
3.
4.
5.
6.
7.
8.
9.

Your list should have included:

1. The starting and finishing time
2. The date
3. The venue
4. The meeting's objectives
5. The membership of the meeting
6. Items to be dealt with and who is leading on each one
7. Whether the item is for discussion, decision or information
8. Any pre-meeting preparation required
9. The time allocated to each agenda item.

There will be meetings which occur regularly where an agenda published in advance is not practical. This does not preclude the idea of drawing up a participative agenda at the beginning of the meeting, however. The meeting is given a specified time limit and each person attending begins by saying what they want to bring up and how long they think they will need. Once everyone has added their agenda items, you can total the time required. If this exceeds the time allocated, those present negotiate either to reduce the time for some items, to defer them altogether, or to lengthen the meeting to accommodate everyone's agenda items. You can have the agenda on a flipchart for people to write on their items as they arrive so that everyone can see what is proposed. This need not add more than a few minutes to the length of a meeting, particularly if you have an outline agenda prepared in advance for people to use. It will pay dividends in terms of getting through the meeting more effectively.

The same format can be used for the agenda if it is published in advance: it can still appear on a flipchart at the meeting to focus everyone's attention on the matters in hand and to avoid having to bring enough spares for everyone who has mislaid or forgotten theirs. A suggestion for an agenda format is shown below.

AGENDA

Meeting: Date:
                                  Time:
                                  Venue:

Present:

Agenda item   Sponsor   Time   Discuss/decide/inform

Try using the format for some of your future meetings and see if it helps to focus the meeting and save valuable time.

Meeting action notes

Sometimes part of a meeting is taken up with arguing about what was agreed at the previous meeting, even when minutes have been taken. This is clearly not an effective use of your time: you need to have an accurate and simple record of who agreed to do what by when for each meeting. There is little need to record anything other than these facts for most of the meetings you attend at work. Increasingly, even routine staff meetings are minuted and this is sound practice. However, too often too much is minuted in such a way as to lose whatever clarity there may have been in the actual meeting. At some future meeting, time how long is spent arguing over the minutes of the previous one! There is rarely any need to record who said what in most work meetings, although there may be such a need in formal meetings like those of the governing body or the AGM of the parents' association.

The format on the next page is one possible suggestion which would ensure that no one is in any doubt over what was agreed at the meeting. It has the advantage that if the meeting scribe completes the form as things are agreed, it can be photocopied at the end of the meeting and distributed immediately for people to take away with them. No one has any excuse for not knowing and no one has the chore of writing minutes after leaving the meeting. They are agreed before anyone leaves.

MEETING ACTION NOTES

Meeting:		Date:
Those present:		
Who	Will do what	By when
Date of next meeting:		
Venue:		

In planning some meetings, particularly important ones in large organizations, it can help to have a meetings planning checklist to ensure that everything is prepared. How often have you turned up to meetings to find a change of room due to a double booking, not enough chairs, the tables laid out wrongly, no overhead projector and screen which you desperately need for your presentation, and so on? When this is the case, there is an awful lot of wasted time while matters are rectified and the meeting is inevitably less productive than it might have been. Try devising a simple meetings planning sheet along the lines of the following example.

MEETING PLANNING SHEET

Meeting:	Date:
	Time: to
Objectives:	Venue:
	Room reserved
Participants:	Agenda set
	Agenda circulated

Meetings materials:
    paper, pencils
    name cards/badges
    handouts
    other

Equipment:
    Overhead projector
        spare bulb
    Slide projector
        spare lamp
    Flipchart
        pens
    Whiteboard
        pens
        cleaner
    Video machine and TV
    Extension reels

Refreshments: Room layout
    Coffee
    Tea
    Herb tea
    Fruit juice
    Water
    Biscuits

Leading meetings effectively

Having prepared effectively for your meeting you now need to ensure that you do not waste everyone's time by conducting it badly. Let us begin with a self-assessment of your performance in leading meetings.

SELF-ASSESSMENT IN LEADING MEETINGS

How effective are you at: 6 = excellent

Starting on time?	1	2	3	4	5	6
Encouraging discussion?	1	2	3	4	5	6
Keeping to the agenda?	1	2	3	4	5	6
Clarifying views?	1	2	3	4	5	6
Drawing out the less confident?	1	2	3	4	5	6
Preventing people from dominating?	1	2	3	4	5	6
Summarizing what has been agreed?	1	2	3	4	5	6
Maintaining a balance of views?	1	2	3	4	5	6
Ensuring expert advice is available?	1	2	3	4	5	6
Checking commitment to decisions?	1	2	3	4	5	6
Ending the meeting on time?	1	2	3	4	5	6

Total score

How did you do?

If you scored 66, you are either an expert at conducting meetings or totally self-deluded.

If you scored between 50 and 66, you are fairly good at conducting meetings but have room to improve.

If you scored between 35 and 50, you are wasting too much of your colleagues' valuable time and need to improve your techniques.

If you scored between 20 and 35, you are wasting a lot of time and should take urgent steps to improve your chairing skills.

If you scored less than 20, you should cease chairing meetings immediately, at least until you have finished this chapter!

Of course this was a self-assessment exercise, and it is always possible that you have not been as honest as you might have been or that you have marked yourself more harshly than is necessary. To get a real view of your effectiveness as a meeting leader, you should ask some of your colleagues, including those that you do not get on with too well, to complete the previous exercise for you.

Rules for effective chairing of meetings

To effectively chair meetings and make the most effective use of the time allocated requires you to follow a few simple rules. These are as follows.

Start on time

To delay the start of the meeting because people are not there is to punish those who turn up on time and reward the late-comers. Once people know that you always start on time regardless, they will be more likely to arrive on time. You could try setting unusual start times like 4.07 or 3.47. This will make people aware that 4 o'clock does not mean 4-ish!

Encourage discussion

If the meeting involves consultation and discussion, you need to encourage people to offer opinions and ideas. Ask general questions to begin with so that anyone may answer. As the discussion develops, you can ask specific questions of the whole group before moving on to asking questions of individuals. Avoid asking questions which require simple yes or no answers if you are trying to promote discussion.

Keep to the agenda

If the attendees have had an input into the agenda, they should be more committed to sticking to it. Be assertive enough to bring people back to the item under discussion if they are tempted to stray away from it.

Clarify poorly expressed views

Some people will express themselves less clearly than others and your job as conductor of the meeting is to clarify what they mean so that the rest of the group understand and a debate does not begin. Be sure to clarify what has been said, and check for agreement from the person involved that you clarified rather than said what you wished they had said!

Draw out the less-confident

There will be those at any meeting who are shy of speaking and need to be supported. In order to avoid much time-wasting after the meeting as people discuss what they really feel in corridors, encourage them to express themselves in the meeting. Once the discussion is under way, ask them direct questions – avoid this early on as it may unnerve them. Try sitting the least confident person next to you so that you can hear their contributions and, if need be, repeat them for the rest of the group.

Prevent the over confident from dominating the meeting

You need to be assertive and point out that it is time to hear from someone else. Ask another individual to give her/his view.

Summarize what has been agreed

The more effectively you can summarize what has been agreed on each item, the more effectively the scribe can record decisions on the action notes sheet for distribution at the end of the meeting.

Maintain a balance of views

If you find speakers are simply repeating what others have already said, there is no point in continuing the discussion on that issue. Ask if anyone has a different view to express and if no one has, move to a decision. You could play devil's advocate yourself and put a contrary point of view to check the commitment of the meeting to the one being openly expressed.

Ensuring expert advice is available

There will be meetings where you need to pass on information that is fairly technical or with which you are not particularly familiar. You have two choices: swot up on the information and hope that no one asks about anything you might have missed; or invite along someone who is an expert on the subject and save yourself a lot of time. When explaining some curriculum matters to the governing body or the parents, for instance, the sensible option is to invite the curriculum coordinator to that part of the meeting to give the presentation and answer questions. Another example would be inviting an OFSTED inspector to talk to staff about inspections rather than trying to do it yourself.

Check commitment to decisions

Having someone transcribe ensures that all decisions are recorded. Before they are recorded you need to seek the agreement of those present that what you think has been agreed is what they think was agreed. Silence might not mean assent.

End the meeting on time

Having an agenda which has timed items should mean the meeting running to time. It also means that you can be aware of any over-running and seek agreement as the meeting progresses on how to cope with it. Make sure that you sit facing the clock so that you can wind up each item on time subtly, without constant reference to your watch.

Being an effective participant in meetings

In some meetings time is wasted because some of the participants are not adequately prepared or organized. How effective are you in meetings? Try the following self-assessment exercise to see.

SELF-ASSESSMENT IN PARTICIPATING IN MEETINGS

How effective are you at:

Arriving on time?	1	2	3	4	5	6
Being familiar with the agenda?	1	2	3	4	5	6
Reading papers in advance?	1	2	3	4	5	6
Thinking through various options?	1	2	3	4	5	6
Keeping to the point?	1	2	3	4	5	6
Responding to points rather than personalities?	1	2	3	4	5	6
Preparing for the items you will lead on?	1	2	3	4	5	6

Total score

How did you do?

If you scored 42, you are a model meetings person and never waste a minute of any meeting you attend.

If you scored between 32 and 42, people must be pleased to have you in their meetings as you are so well prepared.

If you scored between 22 and 32, you waste some time in meetings and need to set about improving your performance.

If you scored between 12 and 22, you must annoy a lot of people by wasting time in their meetings.

If you scored less than 12, don't even think of attending another meeting until you have learned to prepare effectively for them!

Rules for being an effective meetings participant

To participate effectively in meetings and avoid being the cause of much timewasting within them, you need to keep to the following simple rules.

Arrive on time

This does not mean dashing in one second before the meeting starts, but arriving in time to arrange any papers you need, to check any equipment you may be using, and to see anyone with whom you need to check things before the meeting begins.

Be familiar with the agenda

Make sure that have read the agenda before the meeting and are aware of whether you need to be there at all or for only part of the meeting. Being familiar with the agenda should also ensure that you have the correct papers with you.

Read papers in advance of the meeting

You can waste an awful lot of other people's time by holding up the meeting while you read some document that you have had for a fortnight. Make sure that you have read the papers in advance and highlighted any significant points you may want to refer to in the meeting.

Think things through in advance

Having read the agenda and the paperwork associated with the meeting, you should be in a position to begin formulating views on the matters under discussion. This means that you should be able to express them with some clarity in the meeting. This does *not* mean that you cannot modify your views in the light of the discussion, of course.

Keep to the point

Stick to the point at issue and don't be tempted to go off into an interesting (to you) anecdote which is barely relevant.

Knowing the agenda and the paperwork should help you to avoid the worst excesses here.

Respond to points rather than to personalities

Make sure that you address what is being said rather than responding to who is saying it. It is all too easy to agree with people you like and to argue against those with whom you do not get on. Ask yourself how you might respond to a particular argument if it were put by someone else.

Prepare properly for items that you will lead on

If you are to lead on a particular item, make sure that you are well prepared. Have all your material, handouts and visual aids ready and anticipate the questions you might get.

If you try to improve each of these areas, you should find yourself growing in popularity as you attend meetings and help them to run more smoothly and effectively, saving time for everyone.

CHAPTER 8
Summary and Review

We began by looking at why teachers need a book on time management and how poor time management actually costs the school money. You did an analysis of how effectively you use your time at present before looking at, and trying, ways of assessing more accurately your use of time through keeping time-logs. This enabled you to identify your particular timewasters and set your priorities for improving your time-management skills.

We then looked at the importance of effective planning and you tried out some practical ideas to help you with long-, medium- and short-term planning. You looked at the importance of distinguishing between urgent and important tasks and how to prioritize them effectively by considering the impact of each task on your pupils' learning.

Next we looked at how effective classroom organization can reap rewards by saving time and having a major impact on your pupils' learning. You looked at the way matching your teaching to all four learning styles (activist, pragmatist, reflector and theorist) can help to save time by making learning more accessible to more pupils first time around instead of having to repeat yourself. You learned how to notice the sensory preferences of your pupils and to communicate in such a way that they all listen effectively. You then considered some simple strategies for organizing your non-teaching tasks more effectively, including having your workspace well organized, with a place for everything and everything in its place.

Paperwork has increased in the teaching profession and you learned that there are only four possible ways to deal with it: act on it, pass it on, file it or bin it. You assessed the need for filing papers and were encouraged to review the effectiveness of your current filing system.

The final section was on the thorny question of meetings. Having listed those meetings you attend, you then listed them according to their impact on pupils' learning. You looked at the importance of effective planning for successful meetings, including having realistic and understood objectives, considering the alternatives, and inviting only those who need to attend. An agenda outline was then given which could be used for advance notice or for compiling an agenda at the beginning of a meeting. A simple way of recording the decisions and responsibilities arising from meetings was offered in place of the usual minutes, and you then considered a plan for organizing effective meetings. Having assessed yourself as a meetings leader and as a participant, you then considered a variety of strategies for improving your performance in both respects.

This book should have given you an opportunity to assess your own effectiveness in terms of how you use your time. It has also offered you the tools to help you to use your time well. However, reading this book will not help you to manage your time better unless you actually *do* something to apply what you have learned! If you have completed the exercises throughout, you should already be seeing some improvements. Do remember, however, that any savings plan requires you to make initial sacrifices to gain future benefits. A few minutes spent now in effectively planning your work or organizing your workspace will pay dividends in the future.